A Monkey Prays

A Monkey Prays

*

Ingrid Lynch

Although based on a teacher's real life, this is a work of fiction.

Copyright © 2015 Ingrid Lynch
All rights reserved.

ISBN: 1515356426
ISBN 13: 9781515356424
Library of Congress Control Number: 2015912775
CreateSpace Independent Publishing Platform
North Charleston, South Carolina

*

Prayer is a powerful force. Yet, when it comes to that, I am like some pitiful monkey who's imitating what it's seen others do, likely to fall asleep in the middle of it all. There are dividing lines between what I thought to do and what I ought to do, and between where I succeed and where I fail. These bits and pieces of writing lay out the patterns of my life in the hope other monkeys will read and have a care, perhaps a tear.

Or a laugh.

*

Like Mark Twain, I don't believe in ghosts, but I'm afraid of them. I've been startled by what I guess are ghosts. The first time such a thing happened, it was because of my mother's death. My thyroid picked that stressful time to make my size 10 body quit being me. My husband, Jamie, our small son, and I moved to Florida and were staying with my parents. I had no time to shop, nor much money, either, and Mom's closet was handy. Her clothes fit. I picked one of her blouses to wear when I visited my dying mom in the hospital.

Not a good idea. "Isn't that my blouse?" she asked. Indeed it was. "Well, I guess soon enough you'll have all my clothes," she said sadly, with just a touch of anger.

After her death, I was alone in the viewing room with her casket. I was wearing a black dress of hers. Her body lay in the open casket, wearing a dress she and I had picked for her to wear at my brother's wedding. There were baskets of flowers at both ends of the casket and all around her.

When I approached, I felt a sudden pain on the shin of my left leg. I could see there was a wound of some tiny sort, bleeding beneath the panty hose. Later, someone suggested there must have been an insect from the flowers that bit me. Not so. I retreated to the bathroom and took the pantyhose off. There was no crushed insect in my shoe or under it, and there was nothing on the inside or outside of the pantyhose. Put back together again, I found nothing around the casket or under it. I know I looked carefully. Nothing. There was a wound that looked as if a small fingernail had scraped skin off my leg, and yet there was no snag or torn place on the panty hose. How could that be? I decided that having a daughter come to her viewing wearing one of her dresses was too much for Mom, and she was teaching me a lesson. No other explanation satisfied me. I spoke to her: "Nothing I have fits me anymore, Mom." I hope she heard.

Things happened when Jamie died. He struggled against cancer for years, but the disease won, and he died at home, with hospice helping us. No one ever fought harder against dying than Jamie did.

A day after his death, I paused at the entrance of the room where he died. We had removed everything to accommodate the hospital bed and other equipment hospice needed. It hurt to look at it. As I fled down the hall, I heard a muffled cry of anguish from that room. Is it, then, that the dead linger for a while? Could they throw a book at us, conk us on the head with it? Could they hurl themselves at us, possess us? Follow us around? Should we break into the graves and take our dead out for a drive now and then to keep them happy? Never mind answers; the questions alone scare me.

I took pain killers into his room to help Jamie at all hours of the night, and after his death, I couldn't sleep well in my bed. I settled for naps on the living room sofa. I was almost asleep on the sofa when I heard Jamie speak my name. It was his voice, full of emotion and love. The voice left no mistake about its location. I could tell exactly where he must have been standing, and from what height above me that voice came. "I heard that!" I exclaimed. "You came to tell me goodbye!" It was no half dream from which I roused myself. It happened.

Family ghosts aren't the worst. It's all those other things out there. Years ago, at a place in Scotland called Glencoe, I tromped into a valley between mountains with my water colors, brushes and inks, paper, and a drawing board. I could see the old overgrown foundations of cottages around me, so I knew there once had been a village there. The longer I worked with my paints, the sadder I got. Sorrow had that place as its own. There were cars passing on a nearby road, so I wasn't afraid, though perhaps I should have been. At the inn where I was staying, I noticed a book in the owner's small library titled *Glencoe*. He let me read it. I discovered I had been doing my work where once a massacre happened, perhaps close to the spot where bodies had been stacked. This was a valley of tears where some people heard weeping, and if the mist came down from the mountains, the chieftain's ghost could be seen, local people said, complete with the feathers on his cap and the knife in his back. What in the world was I doing there, crossing the line between the living and the dead? Good grief.

Maybe that's why prayers are so important, and why we keep animals around us to tie us more securely to being alive. I think we can sense when someone is praying for us, and God knows we poor monkeys need all the help we can get, with all those things we can't see or understand around us.

*

I wrote a note to a rural dad, mentioning that his son, my student, had a strong body odor. I asked for cleaner habits. Here's the note that came to me from that dad:

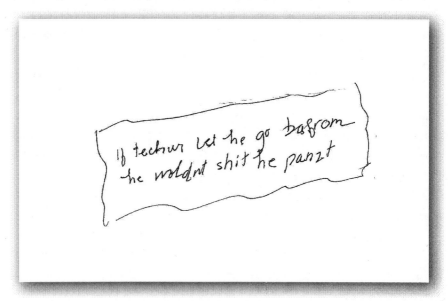

Well, he spelled *shit* right.

*

I know Shakespeare said a rose would smell the same no matter what we call it, but he never taught over 150 middle school students a day, and he never had a seating chart with all their names on it. Whatever else can be said of me, I do know names, lots of them. My seating charts were filled with names that sounded much alike: Larry, Terry, Mary, Susie, Debbie, you know. When a Biblical name came in, or any spelling variation of one, no matter how it was spelled, I was glad to get it. I would put "Hezaciah" on my seatng chart as "Hezzie," and I would learn his name first. God bless the names that come from God.

Names of African-American families were more memorable than others. I welcomed Pansy and Gardenia, although Gardenia White was among the darkest skinned students I ever taught, and I wondered if her name gave her any emotional problems. Did the girl named Cadenza come from a musical family, I wondered? How about Cementia? Was there a worker from some construction site that fathered her? Latoya always gave my tongue problems, and I came close to calling her Toyota.

Hippies gave names they loved, but I wonder how the children felt about being named, as three from one family were: Rivers, Mountains and Plains. Imagine being a full-breasted girl named Mountains.

One family named their children after the states in which they were born, as sort of a family history. Cal was California, Al was Alabama, and Mo was a girl born in Missouri. I played with the thought that if they had a son born in Utah, he would be a little short fellow called Ute. And what was the red-haired family of Irish descent, last name Carey, thinking of when they named their son Harry? Did he grow up to be suicidal?

Then there're last names usually first names. The James family was one of those. Their identical twins were so alike they even dressed alike and finished each other's sentences. Only their cowlicks gave them away. One had a cowlick perched on his forehead that went thisaway, and the other's went thataway. Their names? Ronald Donald James and Donald Ronald James. What were the parents thinking?

Some names are gender-less: Robin, Bobby, Toni, Jamie, Sydney. Any of those could be a skinny, flat-chested girl with short hair and a deeper voice, or a boy with longer hair and a higher voice. Shakespeare didn't know diddley squat.

*

My family avoided the word "black" and preferred "colored" when speaking of Americans of African descent. Well, black has a—ha ha—dark past. There's devil's food cake, and the villain is twirling his black moustache and wearing his black hat, not to mention black magic and black death.

I never felt using the word "colored" was something racial till I had to deal with a form I had to fill out about the students. For it, I had to question them about their race. Some of the questions were stupid (are any of you Polynesian?), but it was when I asked them to raise their hands if they were colored that I ran afoul of the dreaded racism. One kid protested. "Don't call me colored," he said, "I ain't polka dotted." Keeping in mind how many students will color everything polka dotted if asked to "color" anything, I politely said, "Well, what do you want me to call you, then?"

"I want you to call me Sam," he said.

Oh, wise Sam. Wiser than the teacher, who wondered what would happen if she just wrote on that form "Forget this crap. They're kids."

Sam made me dislike him a moment later. "What would you call me if my daddy was white?" What are you, some kind of smart ass, Sam?

Problem was, Sam reminded me of myself, in a strange way. I remembered myself as a child asking my grandfather, "If you don't trust colored people, then why is it when I get left behind, you always call Miss Tishee to come take care of me?" (Miss Tishee was a colored lady named Letitia). Or, "If you don't trust colored people, Grandpop, how come you have them in the kitchen cookin' the food? They could be spittin' tobacco juice into the biscuit batter for all you know. If they were in the dining room, you could say, 'I'm keepin' my eye on you.' " Or, "Grandpop, why do we go to the beach then, anyways, tryin' to get brown?" Sometimes there was a reply—something about shutting up and eating my beans or a muttering about how if I couldn't be pretty, could I at least be quiet? There were people who would tell you without cracking a smile that they remembered fondly the days when you weren't anybody if you didn't have horses and slaves. I was considered some sort of liberal.

Today, even though I'm the same person with the same outlook, I'm considered a conservative. Go figure.

Sam gave me problems in the classroom, and I never let him get away with anything. As a result, Sam told me his mamma was going to come into school and beat me up. "My mamma says she's gonna come in here and beat you up," he threatened.

"That's going to happen soon, then," I countered, "because there's a parent conference night coming up end of this week." Sure enough, on that night, Sam's mom showed up. She was a delightful woman, and I had a good talk with her. Next school morning, I told Sam that. "Met your mom, Sam, and she's not going to beat me up. How's about that, now?"

There was some glaring and some muttering, and finally Sam came up with a final threat, something that would defend him from me, no matter what.

"I've got a dog," he said.

*

Every faculty has its jokester. Ours was Bob. He looked like the skinny half of Laurel and Hardy, the one whose eyes would get big and then he'd cry. I had been out sick, and now he told me that during my absence, my team had a new student, a girl, whom I would meet fifth period this very day.

"Her mother heard a name in the hospital I guess she thought sounded musical. We call her 'Gina'. But her name is Vagina." He said this seriously. Nah, nah, not buying that, Bob. "Oh," he said, "but it's true. And it gets worse next week. That's when they're going to enroll her brother, Rectum."

He tried again later when he sent me a note informing me that a new girl would be joining my fifth period class with the last name "Sass." He warned me in his note to be careful how I pronounced it. Of course, there was no student showing up, and by then I had already figured out that no matter what student that last name was hooked up with, it became a catastrophe (Mary Sass, Donald Sass—it was always going to be *somebody's* ass).

*

There was a flurry of complaints from Sam and students like him, wanting to have a flag of the country of Africa in the classroom. And Sam wanted to be able to use the word "nigger" on others of his race, but no whites could use it. Now I had to emphasize no name calling, not by anybody. Sam responded by writing in big bold letters on the back of his jacket NIGER HERE, NIGER THERE, NIGER NIGER EVERYWHERE. He would turn so I had to see this misspelled message. "Now you've done it," I said. "Writing it counts, too, same as talking, and you've called yourself a name and you can't even spell it right. That's the name of a river, Sam, and you've ruined your jacket. And there isn't any country of Africa. Look it up and you'll see I'm right." He and others went to the encyclopedias trying to prove me wrong. Stick around, Shakespeare. There's lots to learn.

A Monkey Prays

*

Tree Dreaming

The big magnolia lets its branches
Dip too close to ground.
Knifed initials necklace its large trunk;
More than one generation must have been
Climbing and carving.
The tree's fleshy blooms, yellow-dusted,
Sit languidly upon dark leaves.
At night I hear the dropping of those leaves,
And the sound is heavy. I dream
I see men closed in battle:
An officer in a mist, on a light horse.
He has a sword in his right hand, and in his left
With gathered reins he carries a magnolia.
I see his face, weathered, fire-hardened leather,
As he leads the charge.
When I awake, I think I have been told
How old trees go to war.

*

"Nigger! Nigger, where you going?" I heard this coming from below my room on the third floor. The campus elementary school children were on their bikes, circling a young dark-skinned man in military khakis. He was waiting for the bus that came to the front of the teachers' college, and the children were taunting him and throwing pebbles at him.

I was about to yell at them, when he snapped to attention, surprising both me and the children into silence. The children, possibly shamed, drifted off. I felt he would relax then, but he didn't. He stayed at attention until the bus appeared and he got on it. Since he didn't know I was watching, this must have been a thing he did for himself, a statement of his own and his country's worth, as much of those things as he knew.

We Americans so often don't come out strongly for what's right until we're boxed in a corner. I was seeing black bravery of the same sort that put red-tailed fighter planes into battle and proved black pilots' patriotism beyond question.

There must be other young Americans just like this young man.

Who knows how lonely and abandoned some young people must feel?

*

Party Ice

The Navaho sound the soft ice makes
Sluffing in glasses on a tray
Is a ring of old Indians round my heart
Muffling the words the people say
For the moment the tray passed

> Those dancers and I
> Were in a tight circle and ready
> to die.

*

I seated my students tallest in the back, shortest in front. Boy girl, boy girl, staggered, so not much socialization. Directly in front of my desk, partially hidden by a row of my books was the tiniest fellow of all. If I try, even now I can see his blue eyes peering over those books, never seeing the bottom of his young face, but always seeing those eyes and his close cropped blond hair. He was quiet, as if intimidated by the other students, all of whom were larger than he was and more vocal. I was protective of my littlest guy, really.

My classroom door had a clear pane in its center, and when I saw the principal's face framed there, usually I could expect problems. Such as this particular day, when his unhappy face appeared. He beckoned, and I went into the hall to see what he wanted.

He wanted one of my male students.

A pudgy sprig of a girl had collapsed in phys. ed., and when she got the attention she needed, it turned out she was pregnant and didn't even know it. And next came the thing that really got my attention. The father of this soon-to-be-born child was sitting in my classroom at that very moment.

I looked to the back of the room. Which one of those louts would that be? Not so, said the principal. "He's that one in the front. The one peeking over your books with his big eyes."

"No," I protested. Little guy was looking at us not knowing he was the topic of our conversation. "Mac, he's just an infant. He's wearing little bitty toddler pants."

"My dear, it's not the pants. It's what's in them. You send him on down to my office."

The class was almost over anyway. So I sent my little guy to the executioner. But after the class left and my planning period began, I couldn't sit there. I headed to Mac's office. I wanted to defend my poor innocent.

I was almost there when I heard his wail, protesting, denying the facts.

"But that can't be!" he was yelping "We used Saramwrap!" I've misspelled that on purpose. But you can imagine how I made a 180 degree turn right there in the hallway and fled back to my classroom. They should make that stuff either a whole lot stickier or a whole lot less sticky, that's what I say.

*

I see the beautiful handwritten autographs in the little bound autograph notebooks of my mother's time, and I marvel at the fancy sentiments her friends wrote to her. No such emphasis on handwriting today, I am sorry to say, missing the beauty of the "John Hancocks" of the time.

But even without the emphasis on beauty, students' handwriting told some things about them. I'd note the way that girl in the corner dotted her *i* in such a big way, the dot looking like a little pumpkin. Fancy hooks decorating some letters and the way the front of the letter *r* reared up – all this came to mean something as I matched up personalities with traits I saw in their handwriting. No wonder some businesses want a job seeker to write a short essay before they hire: is an expert looking at handwriting to see what's lurking there?

There was the handwriting so cramped and small I could hardly see what it said. I decided those students were going to be spies or bank robbers—or, more likely, they didn't want me to see the words they misspelled and their stupid sentence construction. That was sad, because there were correct answers hidden in that tiny writing. It took twice the time to read those papers.

Michael's paper was one of those with the secretive writing. It was a damp, cold evening, not a night when I could take five minutes outside to prepare for it or to shake off the frustration after it. It took turning the paper this way and that way, handling it over and over in my attempts to read it. He had done it in such a way that he needed only one side of the paper, with answers written sideways in the margins, upside down at the end. Good grief. It was at the end that I noticed he had added an even smaller note for me at the very last bit of space, lower right.

The message he wrote: *Don't touch this paper. I got poison ivy all over me.*

*

Sometimes in a shaft of sunlight, I thought I saw in my classroom the profile of an Egyptian queen, as suddenly gone as it appeared. I would look up and catch the sideways glance of an Inca warrior fooling me for a moment or some descendant of Saladin peeking out at me—and then—nothing of the sort.

*

Slowcomotion

Some things are dubious and slight
Like a grey cat on the grey edge of night

The grey yellow side of an old
garden urn
The grey fingering fist of a fid-
dlehead fern
A wisp of a grey pinking moment
of dawn
Blink—it's still there
Though you'd swear that it's
gone.

*

In the days before there were ten sections of the seventh grade instead of five, before there were five sections of slower students instead of just one, I began teaching. Right after lunch, I taught my one and only slow section history and English. There were fewer than thirty students in the class. It was ideal.

And yet it wasn't, for those students were very slow indeed.

History wasn't the problem. They were with me when we knocked off Nero, and they rode with me and the Huns as they crossed Europe and as they buried their leader under a river bed in a casket of gold; when the bell rang, they didn't want to leave. But oh, English was a different story. What misery.

I can see in my mind's eye the row of fellows who sat right against the wall nearest the classroom door. In front was the big fellow I'll call Tim, wearing his overalls and his work boots. He was a farm boy of that area, not able to spell at all. At one point, I had broken the word *wife* down to the letter *i*, and he couldn't identify even that. In desperation, I said, "You have two of them," recoiling in horror a moment later, realizing how many things he had two of. Buddy, two seats behind him, saved the day by getting Tim's attention and pointing at his eye, and Tim said the proper thing. I had already been amazed that if they recognized *ate* and recognized *late*, if I put a *p* in front and made it *plate,* they would say *dish*. Ditto for *arm,* which they identified, but if I put *f in* front of that, they wouldn't say *farm*, they'd say that was *ranch*. I finally realized this must come from flash card teaching of spelling. But if this was the cause of Tim's problems with spelling, Heaven only knew.

Behind Tim sat a student I came to call (in my mind) Shrimp, for he was as small as Tim was big. Shrimp wasn't his real name, of course. He wore the thickest glasses I ever saw. His eyes were normal in size till he put on those glasses. Once they were on, his face became an owl cartoon. He stuttered, and it was serous stuttering once he got started. He protested everything.

Behind Shrimp sat the student I called Buddy. He was intelligent, hiding his smarts behind an elfin handsome face. He was trouble, capital T.

And behind Buddy sat a tragic, soft-spoken student who lived with his family in a cabin in the rural woods. He seldom spoke.

The day I remember so well came with one of the early spelling tests. We would go 'round the room spelling the words aloud, one student at a time, warming up, and then we would take the test. Each student took a different word, and we would go 'round and 'round, once or twice, till I felt they were ready. And then the test.

When it came to be Tim's turn, he got the word *shirt.* It was good that he got most of it right, but unfortunate that his spelling was a slow drawl S-H-I-T. The class erupted in laughter. "You can tell that's not right," I said. "We'll go around again, and you try that same word again, Tim." So around we went again. And once again, Tim, not remembering how he spelled it the first time, said slowly and loudly S-H-I-T. Laughter again.

"You said that before, Tim," I reminded him. "We'll go around again, and you try again."

I saw Buddy whisper something to Shrimp, and Shrimp pass it on to Tim, so I guessed they told him there was an *r* in there. I dared to hope. Presently, it came to Tim again. This time he said in the most confident of tones S-**R**- H-I-T.

The class laughed. Except for Shrimp. He exploded, banging his small fist against his desk, protesting, "N-N-N-ow y-you've g-g-got h-h-him s-s-s-so screwed u-up, he c-can't even s-spell SHIT right no more!"

And so ended the spelling lesson that day.

*

I love the way teenagers laugh. It echoes down the school hallways like a school of silvery tropical fish, gleaming, glistening, wiggling, giggling notes turning together simultaneously. All in a flash. It always made me smile to hear them laugh. It's one of the things I miss.

*

The questions they can ask! Henry, whose parents were killed in an auto accident, asked why it was they died and he did not. He too, was involved, but he—a tiny infant then—survived. Why was it that the baby survived? How to answer that? I remember I said it could be, though I wasn't a doctor and wasn't sure, that a small baby, so padded with baby fat and pliable, could bounce around in an accident and adults, so much bigger and more brittle, could not. He nodded and seemed to think that made sense. Rachel, whose beloved big dog recently died, wanted to know why it was that God made the pets die ahead of their owners … and was her cat going to die before she did, too? Well, now, I answered, about cats you never know. They do so much whatever whichaway they want to, including dying. But for big dogs I thought I knew something about that, having owned and loved a huge Newfoundland. I told her (and I am sure of this answer) that the big dogs love so deeply that if an owner died before that big dog did, that poor dog would spend the rest of its life suffering, sorrowing. So God arranged it so the big dog would die first, ahead of its owner. I told her little dogs were the toughest of all, and they sorrowed, too, but they were like the cats, working things out on their own. But the big dogs … well, they were what they were.

And as I answered her, I could almost feel my Newfoundland's head resting on my foot as he lay so sick under the table. I had to choke back a tear. Those dear gentle giants don't live as long as other dogs. They take a bit of your heart with them when they go.

*

Cats Ask

> Cats ask a brief question when
> wakened
> It's a "You, again?"
> All in one uplifted
> Throat Note.

*

Shrimp liked to steal pens. This put him in direct competition with me. I had no motive, except I was always using pens, and so when I saw one lying about I supposed it was one of mine

I had left out, so I took it. Shrimp, on the other hand, liked to take other students' possessions. He always stuck his stolen pens down the front of his pants into his underwear. He knew I wouldn't be taking him out into the hall, telling him to unzipper because I was going in there to get that pen out. So there was a lot of rolling of eyes when others complained about Shrimp, and he got away with pens a lot.

On this day, however, I was having Shrimp and his friend Pudge give out some pages I should have given out earlier. The class was soon ending, and so I gave Shrimp a little nudge to get him started. "The bell is going to ring soon," I told him, and I pushed him a little. Remember now, Pudge was close to him on his right, I was sort of beside him and behind him on his left, and the row he was to give the papers to was right up against his leg. How much of a shove could I have given him, eh? As they were leaving the classroom, I did hear Pudge say to him, "You better tell her about that pen." I supposed Shrimp had done his pen thing again.

That evening, at home, I got a call from the school nurse, a kindly woman named Millicent who came in several times a week, part time, all our school could afford. Of course she knew me and my phone number. Everybody knew everybody in the school. Staff never changed, and students came from the same families year after year. "Maurice (Shrimp's real name) told me you pushed him hard in class today," she said. Wait a minute, no I never did any such thing. "Well, he says you did," she continued, and in my mind's eye I could see her kind face frowning. "You'd better hope that safety pin stays shut all the way out of his system." Say what? Turned out Pudge was referring to a closed safety pin Shrimp had in his mouth ("You better tell her about that pin," was what he really said, not "pen"). When I nudged Shrimp I took him by surprise, and he swallowed the damn thing.

I spent a restless night, you bet. But next day, Millicent told me, midmorning, that Shrimp's pin had exited his body still closed. Glad to hear it, but the news came too late. I was already irritated with Shrimp, possibly because I spent the entire school day sleepy and grumpy. So it came at the worst possible time, when I was looking forward to going home and taking a nap, that an emergency involving Shrimp occurred. It involved behavior on the school bus.

We had two lady bus drivers who were Mennonites. If they had been Amish, they wouldn't have been driving a school bus anyway. But some Mennonites allowed modern transportation, and these ladies were of that sort. They did, however, wear on the back of their heads prim, starched, round, tiny white caps pinned in place, exact center back of the head. Perfect targets for students like Shrimp who saved up orange peelings to throw at those targets.

A few students got carried away with themselves, and I bet Shrimp was among those, and they ended up throwing a whole orange at the target. At least one of these hit the mark, causing the bus to swerve all over the road. The bus ended up back at the front of the school, with its door shut tight. The principal was already on hand at the side of the bus when we teachers were about to leave. Now we were summoned to the side of the bus. "These smart asses are giving false names," he said. "Please get on the bus, and help me identify them."

Shrimp's name should have been Hitler, but he chose Tinkle Bell as his new name. When I identified him and told him to get off the bus, he unwisely decided to defy me. Big mistake. I was young and strong then, and before I even knew I was doing it, I had seized Shrimp AKA Maurice AKA Tinkle Bell and hoisted him into the air. The other students on the bus sat open mouthed and staring as I packed the kicking and squalling one under one arm and propelled him onto the pavement.

The principal got hold of him by his collar and was almost into the building when Shrimp's mom arrived, parking her car in front of the school, just in time to see Shrimp in tow.

This was a mamma terrier who had somehow sensed trouble on the bus when no bus arrived, and she came to see what was up. Just in time to see Mac The Principal yanking and snatching a protesting Shrimp ... Maurice. She followed the principal into the building. I followed her, in case the principal needed some back-up. I didn't realize Mac was unaware of her behind him. He went into his office and slammed the door behind him. The door knob hit mama in the stomach. Ouch.

The other students got off the bus in silence. The next day, the rumor went around that Shrimp had been beat up, and his mom had been kicked in the stomach, and she was going to sue that mean old man and me for sure. But nothing came of it.

*

Not quite true, for one thing did come from it. The very next day, Shrimp was so puffed up with self- importance, I took him out into the hall for a "discussion." Today, I surely would have been fired for what I did. Shrimp and I did a sort of dance, with me slinging him into the lockers—like this: "You will quit being so rotten on the bus and in the classroom, do you hear?"—BANG BANG—"And stop stealing and calling people names"—BANG BANG—"And if you keep it up, I can drag you out here again"—BANG BANG BANG—"And I don't care what you tell the nurse or your mom ... or anybody else ... because you've been so bad in all your classes, there's at least three teachers I know will say"—BANG BANG—"they were right here with me and all we did was talk." I told him even if he ripped his clothes and said I did that, I didn't care; that only meant I would hurt him, and other teachers would back me up. For about a week and a half, Shrimp was actually good. Then it wore off.

We had an assembly. I told the students not to chew gum. Among them was a fellow named Wayne, who always seemed to have a toothpick hanging out of his mouth. He and Shrimp were sitting in the middle of a row, so I couldn't have gotten to them no matter how much I wanted to. About half way through the program, because I was keeping my eye on that twosome, I saw Shrimp pass a stick of gum to Wayne. Shortly after, Wayne was having a good time with that gum, puffing it out in bubbles, sucking it in, popping it loudly. Shrimp was delighted. Somebody else was going to catch it, while he, smart aleck Shrimp, wouldn't get any blame at all. When the assembly was over, I caught Wayne and Shrimp and stopped their whole row dead in its tracks.

"I know Shrimp gave you that gum, Wayne, so this is not entirely your fault." I put a tissue in the palm of my hand. "Give me that gum," I said, indicating the piece of tissue. Wayne pushed the piece of tissue aside. Then he ground the gum into my palm. Shrimp appeared to be thunder struck with admiration. Without even thinking, my arm came up, my hand flew at Wayne's head, and I was quite surprised to see I had stuck that gum into his hairline. And once I realized that, I took care to grind it in. Oh, it felt good, I must say. And Shrimp was about to faint.

I was sure I would hear about that. I never did. Wayne reported to school the very next day with a good chunk of front hair missing. Nary a word from home. I can only suppose he was a rotten apple there, too. But that was surely a reason to sue me. Didn't happen. It was a different time, back then. Somebody just sat on it, I suppose.

*

I mentally admitted defeat with Shrimp. It was time to ask for a schedule change. When Shrimp realized I was going to ask that he be dumped from my class, he was stunned. No, no, he didn't want that. He promised to be better, and to my surprise he was. So I kept him, knowing his improvement couldn't last forever.

Buddy often picked on him. On one occasion Buddy put a girly magazine in Shrimp's hands, upside down, and made fun of his eyesight. Another occurrence was Buddy's fiction that Shrimp had been born when a comet passed and would die, surely, when another comet passed our planet, for that was (according to Buddy) how things worked. This got Shrimp so upset I put Buddy into the restroom for a time out.

My classroom was in a section of the school that once had elementary classes, and my students had a restroom included right inside the classroom. The toilets were low to the floor, so we didn't use it at all. I told Buddy to pull down the seat and stay there till I said he could come out.

And then I forgot him entirely. He sat there silently throughout the rest of the afternoon, happy as he could be, missing all his afternoon classes. Now it was Shrimp who reminded me, as students were leaving for the day, that Buddy was still with me. "Y-Y-Y-you f-f-fergot B-B-B-Buddy," he said, looking very concerned. And there sat Buddy with a big grin on his face. I should have been fired, as I already said.

Later on, I heard Buddy fought in Vietnam. I felt sorry for the Cong.

*

If you wonder what students remember, I can tell you. A student I had taught years earlier reminded me of it. When I recognized her and asked her how she was doing, she said she was doing well, and she certainly remembered me, and would I want to know why she remembered me so well, above all other teachers she ever had? It was because at the end of the year, I was giving out awards, and I tried to give everybody in the class an award for something or other, even if it was for something humorous. "You gave me the award for having the best smile," she said. Even as she said it, she flashed that smile, and I remembered it at once. "I still have that award pinned on my bulletin board," she said, years after I gave it to her.

Tell them something nice about themselves.

*

I helped students after school. I can't remember all of them (certainly not), but there's one I should remember. He was the poorest of them all. In school he was silent, often bullied by kids like Buddy. I gave him boxes of tissues because he always had sinus infections.

I got a good look at his home because I drove him there and entered the place. He lived in a log cabin with both parents and several siblings. There was no electricity (they used kerosene lamps). Water came from an artesian well with a bucket. The whole place smelled bad, possibly because there was an outhouse but nothing else I could see for cleanliness.

The parents were semi-literate. I had written a note to them, and I suppose they were able to read it. The father responded with a note of his own, and it was a piece of work, but it got his message across. In all, there was disorder, dirt, disease, ignorance and coughs. And missing teeth—that, too.

The boy had a dented bicycle that was a prized possession. The parents told me that and how he would ride and walk it on dirt till he got to the nearest county paved road. He would ride it up and down to his heart's content, since there wasn't much traffic there.

One of our local businessmen was speeding on that road after calling on his customers and having a few too many drinks to celebrate the holidays. He struck the boy and his bike, and then he sped away, trying to convince himself it was just a bump or a dog. At home, he thought better of it and called a state trooper he knew. In the meantime, one of our school custodians who lived nearby discovered the dying boy. The back wheel of his bike was still turning. The boy died in his arms.

As for the businessman, he tried to keep busy. He said he thought he'd hit a deer. Later he fell from the roof he was repairing and died in the hospital.

This was an unlucky white student. Later on, there was another unlucky one, this time a black boy who came for the first day of school, saw that he was in a slow reading group, and never attended the second day of school. Who knows how much ridicule he must have endured all his short life. He went home and committed suicide. Students like these two make a mockery of No Child Left Behind. Neither of them ever had a chance in hell. They were left behind at birth.

*

So Mac The Principal said to me, "You worry too much about your students. You should remember what Confucius says about that." What? I thought perhaps Mac would say "You cannot carve on rotten wood," or some such thing. What he said was, "You have to remember you can't shine shit."

*

What Mac didn't consider was this: it isn't worry that catches up with any teacher who stays in one place long enough to see young lives end. It's grief, not from names on some memorial stone to fallen heroes in battle, though there is that, too, but from what you feel when you hear a *whomp* from across the lake that tells you a car has hit that tree on the curve. The girl who had her hair dyed green for Saint Patrick's Day died there. It's from remembering how a boy sat perched forward on his chair, one leg tucked beneath him, working on a model of a Roman soldier. He left work unfinished on his desk at home to go with friends riding on a rain-slicked road in a car that ended up wrapped around another tree. Three died in that one. I saw the remains of the car and some teeth in the back seat. I also saw his father, who managed the meat section of our supermarket, trying to go on with life, looking like a walking dead man. I heard the boy's room was left untouched, his books still lying on his desk. Nothing Confucius said can touch what parents feel. I attended funerals, and I prayed as hard as any monkey can. But no teacher's grief can touch what parents go through.

*

What I want back is the chance to be more appreciative and to let the people I depended on know how much I loved them. Too late now. I know that. But if I could go back, I'd be so different. And I'd hang on to certain things, important things that somehow disappeared over time. My first husband and I visited an elderly couple related to him. She was blind, and her husband walked with a cane. But they were dressed in their best, anticipating our visit. I was stunned when the husband presented me with two carvings he'd made of farm animals he remembered from his young days on a farm. I praised him, astonished he had gone to so much trouble, but now I wish I'd said more, had spent more time with him, listening about his life on the family farm. Did I write him a note? I expect not. And I remember Sam, in class, saying, "She says you won't wear it." He was talking about a crocheted hat his aunt made as a gift for me. I wore it constantly. Did I ever even write a thank you note to her? Doubtful. Before I die, could I get back my exquisitely carved little pig and my little sheep? And my yellow and white and blue hat? I promise, I promise, to take better care of them. Please ...

*

Maryland Crabs Frying

My grandmother is flouring soft crabs at the sink
And she can see, out the window, clams being opened
The knife flips under the fat little crab bodies
To clean out their bay-brown backs
And the blade cuts away the mouthparts, the eyes
Little "stills" they're called, delicious when fried
Now the bodies twirl in flour, front and back
The back fins promise to be crunchy and crisp
As she places them in the deep hot fat
Fills the waiting pan, checks the limas
Her great coiled braid of chestnut hair bobbing and moving
And the little crabs bubble in the oil
Sounding almost as they did
When they bubbled hidden in the eelgrass

*

There are words I dare not use in the classroom. I must never use *gay* to mean happy, *cock* to mean a rooster, *fairy* to mean a tiny person in the woods, *rubbers* to mean foot coverings to keep your shoes dry, and *balls* to mean anything at all. Also, I must beware of any form of the irregular verb *come*, because it has a sexual meaning, and *lay* or *laid* for the same reason.

I mention this because Buddy at the board has done some work on irregular verbs, and now he is like the conductor of a symphony orchestra, waving a piece of chalk. "I *come* on the train," he says with a sly grin.

The class snickers.

"I *came* on the train. We *all* are *coming* on the train."

The class is amused.

"I *laid* her. She was a good *lay*." Now he's gone too far.

"That's enough, Buddy. Go sit down." But a little later, he raises his hand, and now he's including me in his comedy routine. Clearly, I'm his straight man.

"Is it *stink, stank, stunk*?" he asks.

Yes, I nod.

"Then, is it *shrink, shrank, shrunk*?"

Yes.

"Well, then, is it *think, thank, thunk*?"

No.

"Oh." He pretends disappointment.

The class is following us back and forth as if they're watching a tennis match. I know he's headed for something, just not sure what.

"Well, is it *sing, sang, sung*?"

Yes.

"And is it *ring, rang, rung*?"

Yes.

"Then it's gotta be *bring, brang, brung*, right?"

No.

The class gives a mock moan. I'm intrigued. He's headed for something, and I can see it on his elfin face, as if he's Pan about to ripple a tune off his pipes.

"Is it *sit, sat, sat*?"

Yes.

"Then, it's got to be *spit, spat, spat*, right?"

Yes.

This causes some confusion among his listeners. Amongst them *spit* is used exclusively or *spitted*. I'm sure nobody in the class ever uses *spat*. Or, for that matter, ever heard of the word.

With a flourish he delivers his punchline. "Well, what about *shit, shat, shat*?"

A gasp goes up, similar to what happened in theaters when Clark Gable said he didn't give a damn, the first time a cuss word ever was heard in a movie. Buddy has brought *shit* to the classroom.

For just a moment, a bell rings in my brain. Could that be correct? Somehow, I think maybe it is. I blink. And Buddy catches it, smarty pants that he is. "Is that right?" he asks, eyes wide.

"I'm not sure. But I don't know where we could check on it—"

He is already on his way to the dictionaries. "Buddy, it won't …"

Shrimp has jumped up to join him, and now the two of them are flipping through dictionary pages. I'm watching Shrimp. He's humming, shifting his weight from one foot to the other in a kind of dance to his own humming music. I've seen Shrimp stutter intensely when he's angry or up-tight, and stutter less when he's at ease. When a space suit was on display in the library, Shrimp asked, "How do they p-pee and p-poop?" When at an historic estate, at a roped-off bedroom, Shrimp noticed a piece of furniture beside the bed, and he looked at me, questioning. "It's got a pot in it," I said, "for going to the bathroom at night." "It's too close to the p-piller [pillow]," he replied with very little stuttering.

Now Buddy is walking away. "*Shit* ain't in there," he says.

Here comes Shrimp dancing behind him. "But *bitch* is in there, Buddy. *Bitch* is in there!" And not one trace of stuttering. Which is a bitch, as far as I am concerned. Somebody, someday, must explain that to me.

*

When you are in the sixth grade and not very worldly-wise, you question some things unwisely, don't question others, and you make some mistakes. When my mother took me into the bathroom and showed me how to use a sanitary napkin, there wasn't much explanation for the blood I had on my panties. "Well, now you're a woman," she said sadly. And that was all. I had a question in my mind to ask, something like "Wuzzatmean?" But I could tell from her tone of voice it wasn't something very good. Possibly it meant I was going to die in three months. Who knew? And who had the guts to ask? Not me, for sure. I knew being a woman meant having the children. I had seen dogs coupled together, had a baby brother, so I knew something about male and female differences, about mating, but I had no idea about where babies came out. I figured the babies came out of the belly button. Made sense to me.

Asking the Methodist women in my family was unthinkable. I would have to be drunk to do it; that was another no-no, and I was too young to drink, anyway. Even the word "pregnant" was not used around my grandmother. So I walked around in splendid ignorance.

Until our class took a tour of the hospital, and we came to the delivery room. I guess I thought babies arrived as the mother was standing up (I mean, if they popped out of the belly button, one could catch them as they came out, right?) To this person in the sixth grade, the delivery table meant the female was lying down. Strange. Suspicion began creeping into my small brain. Then I spied the stirrups on each side of that wide table. What? Such an impossible stretch, and it meant one's legs were spread wide apart—really W-I-D-E apart. And that meant all the most southern regions of one's body were there, also spread, and that meant babies weren't coming out from any belly button, but were coming out from somewhere down below. What in the world? Did the baby come from the pee hole or the poop hole? I had no idea there might be some other hole. It had not been heard from, and so if it was there, it must be totally useless.

Nobody else had any questions. I gathered up my courage. I finally asked of the nurse standing by, "Doesn't that hurt, those stirrups so far apart?"

"Oh, honey," she answered sadly, looking oddly a lot like my mother when she announced my womanhood, "by that time, believe me, you don't even care!" What? Now, *what* ? I fell back into an obstinate and hostile silence.

Back home, I ventured to the back of the property, where there was a field surrounded by poplar and cedar trees and an old fence. And there I spoke aloud to God about all this business. Out loud, if you please. And it says a lot that I would rather take on God than my grandmother. "I'm never going to get myself in that pickle!" I said to God. "I'm never going to love anybody, you hear me?" I think I said even more. There was a breeze, and it picked up a bit, making the little poplar leaves twirl—almost as if God was saying, "I hear you, gal, and I'll hold you to that." Of course, I fled the scene.

I wondered, later on, years later, if I put a hex on myself about marriage, about men. It was a vow I came to regret, let's put it that way. I still think babies ought to come from belly buttons. I mean, there's the belly button right in the middle of the part of the body that's stretching. It would be convenient. And standing up would work.

What doesn't work, evidently, in a marriage, might be staying after school to help students, or driving them home, and checking papers every night, or dragging papers with you wherever you go on weekends, and even ruining summers with classes. When you come into a room where you and your husband are visiting and he says, "Here comes the old bag now," you're doomed, even if he's kidding. Maybe you get old, and you never have the time to notice it. I never should have gone out into that field and gotten sassy with God, that's what I'm thinking.

*

I Know

> I know how the wind parts my
> child's hair
> Over the fence as I get a glimpse.
> That one is mine, I say, inwardly
> told,
> Flag of my innocence, strands of
> red gold.

*

I Had

I had a friend who was quite a gardener
Weeded and planted although all the while her
Husband blew smoke rings and tapped on her back
And said she should get something sexy and black
To restore her old charms which were obviously gone
There was this young girl who was turning him on
So, I told Fran, I felt very rightly
About a strange plant that held its rows tightly
And blossomed at night
All red, pink and white
If you tore up its roots, it poisoned your heel
If you broke off its branches your lungs would congeal
And in short it delivered all manner of grief
But it had no defense if you took just one leaf
Which you dried up and sliced; then a needle you'd get
To place minute pieces in each cigarette
He made no pretense, so over the fence
I gave her the gift, which she put in her pocket
Next day Jerry was on the autopsy docket
When next I saw Fran she said very sweetly

He questioned her roots and pruned branches neatly
And there on the sill I saw she had got
A green-budded plant in its own little pot
Lips berry red, skin pink and white
It seemed to me Frances had bloomed over night
With a face that was instantly warm and beguiling
Moving about town and so sweetly smiling
Eyes always open and quietly poking
Of course I immediately gave up smoking.

*

I smoked like a choo choo train, which was another thing that aged me. My students talked me into quitting. They kept a chart on me, and they would give me a crayoned X on days I had smoked a cigarette, a check mark when I hadn't. I didn't have the heart to lie to them. But I came to resent having to tell the truth every single day for weeks on end. I still remember the name of the boy who was the keeper of the crayon. His name was Marvin. Jeeze, I got so I hated the sight of him every morning.

*

There was a time when if you married, chances were you would stay married, perhaps for the children's sakes, if for no other reason. Men wore ties and jackets when they were teaching in the classroom, and women wore skirts and dresses (no pant suits). Faculty members stayed till they retired or died. Every spring when the fields were plowed, Indian arrowheads and artifacts appeared in the furrows, and children brought collections of them to school to show the teacher and their classmates, and sometimes they brought original royal land grants from long ago, still pertaining to their family farms. Things stayed put, mostly, and it was both boring and comforting. If you were a woman, and things suddenly changed, you didn't have many other options for a full life, especially if your children were all grown and your marriage had dried up like an old corn husk.

At a school luncheon, a woman I barely knew sat next to me. She was a library volunteer. I knew about her history (in our town, everybody knew everybody's business), but I never had conversations with her. I was newly married, and all the men in my family were still alive, so when she tugged at my arm and spoke to me, it took me by surprise. Her face was open and vulnerable; her eyes dazed.

"One day you wake up and he isn't there," was what she said abruptly. It was as if she thought perhaps I knew where her husband had gone with his secretary.

After, she spoke no more, but went silent. That was the only thing she said. When my first marriage ended and I saw a closet emptied of its clothes, I thought of her, and after a lengthy second marriage, when I had to empty my dead husband's closet of its contents, I thought of her again. Maybe we should have a placard with a printed slogan on it: "Remember this: one day you wake up and somebody you love is gone forever." So we're warned ahead of time. It might help.

*

Maybe monkeys pray sort of. Maybe they just sigh. They're in a safe place with some favorite food, and they sigh this "prayer" of contentment, and God hears that and knows it's a monkey of His, and that makes God smile. I know you can't fall asleep in the middle of it, for one thing, and I've experienced that sort of praying, a moment of thankfulness. Always it makes me sigh, and it is a sort of prayer, at least I think so.

I experienced such prayerful moments especially with animals I knew well—a cat or Rags, our Newfoundland, for example. One Christmas Eve, I came upon Rags asleep, lying on his back nestled next to our bed, snoring (yes, he did snore) … and what he had with him were the camels from the nativity scene under the Christmas tree. He had no interest in anything else, but for some reason, he wanted the camels to sleep with him. Sigh.

On another occasion, as I took him on a walk, we came upon some orphaned mallard ducklings swimming around in a make-do shallow container filled with water. He literally pulled me behind him as he surged to them and flopped beside their "pond." It was clear to me he was fascinated by these small creatures, and he was trying to figure them out, to define them. His huge head was bowed, unmoving, his eyelashes quivering, and his huge paws kept still as a few ducklings came to explore him. They were climbing over his paws. With one playful swipe he could have squashed them, but he kept as still as he possibly could. He was thinking, and he'd forgotten that his big tongue was hanging out of one side of his mouth. How wonderful God is to make such big dogs gentle. Sigh. I read about a Newfoundland bitch named Mable who was present when a child fell off a high pier. Without giving it a thought, Mable leapt into the water and saved the child from death. After that, unfortunately, Mable enjoyed being a celebrity so much she took to pushing kids off the pier just so she could jump in and "save" them. Obviously a thinker (sigh) who ended up being tied up at her owner's house, wondering what went wrong.

There was a negative side about having a huge dog like Rags. Every summer, I brushed bushels of under-coat from this huge hair-grower of a dog who had both an outer sleek coat and a dense fluffy under coat. I could have made blankets from it all. In addition, fleas loved him, ticks loved him, and he developed "hot spots" from their bites. It required lots of attention: both sides, the top, and the underside.

One day I was tending to the Red Cross part of owning Rags when I discovered an alarming thing. My poor dog had developed two large tumors on his penis. Halfway up his penis shaft, here were these two enlarged things, one on each side. I touched one, and it was hard as rock. Good Lord. I immediately called Jack, an acquaintance who raised dogs. I explained the situation to him.

Did Jack ever tell others about our brief conversation? If I were he, I would have. I can imagine how it went: *Do you know how dumb she is? She said she touched one, and it was hard as a rock. She didn't even know when her dog had a hard on. Behind him, the sound of hysterical laughter.*

From then on, I kept things distanced and impersonal with Rags when he was on his back. Lying like that, his lips were flopped into what could have been an evil, lusty smile. How was one to know? I spoke to him about it, for I knew good and well he was a thinker. "Don't you even think about it, you dirty old man of a dog," I said to him.

He looked too happy, dammit.

*

I wanted my young aunt to marry, and then perhaps I'd get her bedroom, instead of having to sleep on a cot in Grandmother's room. When that actually happened, I joyously began sleeping in the spindle bed in that my aunt's old room.

Problems came with the bed. God only knows how old it was (and still is). A regular mattress had been jammed into its small frame. Obviously, it came from a time when people were smaller. Much later, when I came to own it, I had its sideboards lengthened almost five inches to accommodate a three-quarter length mattress. Except for a few Washingtons and Lincolns, children were given coffee instead of milk as soon as that could happen, and folks just grew up to be shorter. There must have been less of everything.

Fact was, the bed shook violently. I told myself it was because of that mattress, and because the house was old and had settled. But it was a little frightening when it happened. Sometimes I'd feel the blankets, a quilt or a pillow being pulled away.

Eventually I told my grandmother about that bed. "It only happens when bad people sleep in it," she said teasingly. For a change, I had a snappy come-back. "Oh, yeah? Then how come *you* know about it?"

Children sleep heavily, and when the bed awoke me with its dark tricks, I always fell asleep again right away. It was a problem, but not a very big one.

Years later when my grandmother died, the furniture in the house went away in different directions. Some went to this relative, others to another, and some went to the auction house. A few things came to me. The bed was one of them. I was to take it and promise I would never sell it. Nobody wanted that bed, but nobody wanted to say piss on it and give or sell it away. So give it to me. I'd slept in it for years, so I should be used to it.

When I went through a divorce, I found myself sleeping in that bed once more in a new place. Admittedly, I was vulnerable, and my feelings were raw.

One night I awoke full of fear. It was a fear so strong it awakened me. I was aware that a tiny dark blob of a presence, darker than its surrounding darkness, was pulling away from my side, withdrawing. It slipped between the wall and the side of the bed.

Back into the bed? Hello. Wake-up call. What hadn't been a problem now seemed to have become one. How many people died huddled on that bed, anyway? I spoke to it: "Listen, you," I said. "I don't care what I promised. If you ever scare me again, or scare anybody, for that matter, you're out the door and on your way to the auction house. Whoever you are, I know you hear me. You think about that."

Others have slept in it since, and eventually my son took it into his room, a place so small the bed suited him because of its small size. Even when he became so tall his legs and feet stuck out between the spindles, he continued sleeping there peacefully. After he went off to college, his room worked for guests. A few visitors who knew my family would ask timidly before they spent the night, "Is this that old haunted bed?" But once there was a level floor and a proper mattress, the old tricks ended.

I mention all this because once my husband died and I moved, that bed—disassembled, mattress gone—ended up in a storage room connected to my new, smaller home.

Recently my daughter-in-law asked a favor. My granddaughter, the child some say looks like me when I was little, has a small room, and her mom wondered if she could have that bed, even though she'll have to order a special mattress for it. So a part of my old family will come to be useful again for a new small person. I saw it go out the door, that thing I had known for so many years, its head board and foot board, its slats and sideboards. It touched me, leaving my protection, even though I know it's a good thing.

But still ... even as I watched it and all its history with me moving out ...

"You be good, now," I whispered.
"Or else."

*

When I returned tests, it bothered me that Buddy always laughed. His low scores didn't faze him. He smirked.

Finally I dealt with it. "You're laughing about getting a failing grade?"

He shrugged. "I don't care."

"You pretend that. But maybe you couldn't pass a test even if I paid you."

He was interested. "How much would you pay me?" I had him hooked.

"Five dollars. You have to get a high C. First try."

I spent my time teaching them, reviewing them, testing them, and then re-testing them. I thought of Buddy's class as "short-term learners," because they might not pass first time around. Mostly this was because they had no long-term goals down the line. So I gave some tests on the curve, some not, and I always re-tested on harder stuff. Such as the next test, which would cover punctuation, and the infamous *ie-ei* spelling words that so often went against that old rule "*i before e except after c*."

"Okay," he said. "Cash, though." Here was a little dictator who thought I might give him a no-good check.

Next day, in the A.M., as I went to the faculty room for coffee, I spotted Buddy and a circle of friends sitting in the empty cafeteria. They were prepping him for the next test. Interesting. Day before the test, and on the day of the test, same thing, only now at lunch as well as in the A.M.

Buddy got a low B. The class was delighted. I'd hidden the five dollars in the room. It could have been anywhere except under the chairs and desks (too much old gum under there). It took Buddy and five friends he was allowed to choose about ten minutes to find the money I'd taped on the underside of the globe stand over on the window will.

"So … want to bet you can't get an A?"

"How much?"

"Ten dollars."

Yes, I know what professors say. They say students should learn because of the love and the beauty of learning. Bull shit. This was personal. I had to find out something for myself, something I suspected about Buddy. And now the class was caught up in it. They wanted a piece of this action. I wasn't rich enough to include them, but I compromised. If in addition to Buddy getting at least a low A, if nobody else in the class got lower than a D, then I'd add enough points so that everybody else would get a high C, almost a B. Some of the kids had never seen a B in their lives. They went for it.

There were small groups studying in the library, the cafeteria, the classroom. I was astonished. Buddy got a 96. Nobody else got below a 70. Buddy and his crime-for-hire friends found the ten dollars taped underneath the map.

I couldn't resist. "Want to go for 100? I'll go fifteen."

The results took my breath away. Not only did Buddy get 100, but the grades for the entire class were coming up. This time, I hid three five dollar bills in different encyclopedias. It took longer to find them. I'd promised the class B's, but they almost all got B's on their own. I was astonished.

It had to end, of course. I explained to them that I probably could get fired, paying them to learn like that. Just when it got really good … that was the mournful class attitude. They didn't want it to end, of course. For three months, even after I ended it, the effect held strong for the entire class. They all enjoyed better grades. A few began reading encyclopedias, and one girl took to dusting the book shelves.

But after three months or so, the class settled back into being slow. I think there's a secret about making short-term learners long-term learners hidden in there somewhere. It needs work ... but it could be golden.

*

Time was when we called it "junior high," and it was grades seven and eight. The holiday at the middle of the winter we called "Christmas Vacation." We decorated our rooms, and the day before the vacation was wasted. Students wore Santa hats, and nobody cared, and they carried around candy canes and nobody took them away. They also gave gifts to each other and to their teachers, whatever they could afford. There were so many things I didn't need, all to carry home in a box. I can't remember most of those gifts.

But there was one I will always remember. The giver was a girl, a good student from a poor family. She hustled away before I could grab her to thank her, yet I still can see the hunch of her shoulders, her dark hair and faded sweater. It was as if she didn't want me to dwell on how small and cheap it was, those few bobby pins displayed on a piece of cardboard. My hair was long then, and I always needed pins, so it was a good gift for me. And coming from her, a child I would have wanted to be a daughter of my own, it meant more than any of the others. She would be in her fifties now. Perhaps she remembers giving a gift like that, and as she thinks of it at Christmas, maybe she can sense I think of it, too.

*

There are lines a teacher isn't supposed to cross. You're supposed to protect your students, and that means all of them.

You can't hurt one of them, not deliberately, even if you think he deserves it. If you cross that line …

One of our local men, a tall, handsome fellow, came back from WWII with a European bride. She was an attractive, petite, soft-spoken woman who wasn't saluting the American flag just yet, but she promised to do so pretty soon. As a member of the Resistance, she'd fought against the Nazis, and I'm pretty sure she missed her native country.

The son of this attractive couple was in my first morning class. I'll call him Pierre (not his real name). He was tall, ungainly, and carried with him wherever he went a huge, heavy leather briefcase full of his stuff. I was never sure why he did that, but it was an integral part of Pierre every morning.

In that same class sat the son of the owner of our local building supply and lumber company, one of the more prosperous families in the community. His name was Robert, and he was one of those kids my grandmother would have called a piss ant, full of himself. He became Pierre's tormentor, always ridiculing the way he walked, his appearance and, most of all, his stuffed-full briefcase. Pierre was miserable, and everybody in the classroom, including me, knew it.

I talked to Pierre outside in the hallway. I asked him why he didn't defend himself. "If you don't," I said, "he's just going to pick on you all year."

Pierre was as polite as could be. His mamma didn't want him to fight, and that was that. I was a little surprised to hear that, and I told Pierre so. I told him I knew for sure she fought with all her heart and soul when her country was being picked on. She stood up to the invaders and took risks. "And besides," I said, (and here is where I certainly crossed that line a teacher should avoid), "your mamma doesn't have to know everything, you know."

It may have been the very next morning that Pierre stood up for himself. I was standing outside the classroom right beside the door. As Pierre came down the hall, Robert was approaching from the other direction, and he started in with the insults even before he got close to the door and Pierre. But now something was different. Pierre didn't head into the room as usual. He came to the door, and he paused—just long enough for Robert's head to come within range, is what I'm thinking. I can't describe how that briefcase sounded when it hit Robert's noggin. Maybe the sound a demolition ball makes when it smacks a brick wall would come close. Robert hit the hall floor, out cold. I sent Pierre into the room at once, for Robert was looking kind of like a corpse, and Pierre's wide eyes said he knew that just as well as I did. There was the possibility in both our minds that Robert was a goner.

I was so frightened at the sight of Robert on the floor I almost fainted. I had caused this, of that I was sure. But I got lucky. Robert came around after a bit of my fluttering around him, fanning him, and saying encouraging words I can't remember. I do remember encouraging Robert to keep it in mind in the future that Pierre was armed and out of patience. The problem ended, and peace prevailed. But I made a mental note not to meddle anymore with things that could result in murder, for God's sake.

I mention all this because there came an autumn day, years later, when I was planting some daffodils on the wooded side of my home, and I was interrupted by a tall, handsome man; it was Pierre. His family had relocated to Europe, eventually, and now this young engineer was visiting his father's family. He'd decided to stop by and speak to me. I got to see the "finished" product, a confident adult. With no briefcase.

*

We took a week or so each month for non-fiction oral book reports. Students picked any person, living or dead, or any true incident. They brought the book and an illustration they made, and they tried to talk for at least five minutes. Any person meant any person. If a student chose Hitler, so what? He or she could do that.

In one class was Jess, a light-skinned student of African ancestry. Since the beginning of the school year, Jess had worn a big X hanging on a chain around his neck. So it was no surprise when he chose to do his oral book report on Malcolm X. No problem. Right?

Wrong.

Here came two white male students, protesting Jess's choice. "Malcolm X wanted to kill white people," they said. Suddenly, even though they'd seen it for quite some time, they were offended by the big X.

"If he can wear that X as a sign of Malcolm X, then we can choose Robert E. Lee as our report, and we can bring a Confederate flag to school for General Lee." They intended to each take a part of Lee's life, breaking their project into two talks, and each would do half of the work on a poster.

Then their fun began. They followed Jess around, flapping their miniature Confederate flags at him. Not one big flag, but several little ones were what they favored. Jess would look up in the middle of a class, and there one of them would be, at that window pane in the middle of the classroom door, wiggling it at him. They took turns messing with him, and they yakked it up all round the school how Jess was a disciple of a white-hater. It began to bother everybody; it became a white versus black thing. Talking to them about Jess's rights didn't work.

I got called to the office of Mac The Principal.

"How's about calling off the Civil War in 8B and do it the sooner the better?" was what he said.

I called in Jess and the other two. It was an unfriendly meeting.

"He can keep that X as long as he wants," I said. "It never bothered anybody before you two started in on him. You brought the flags to school, though, just to start trouble. No more Confederate flags in the school or on school property."

"You hate white people!"

"I'm white myself, dummy. You know that's not true. When Malcolm X went to Mecca, he saw Muslims of all kinds getting along. Maybe that gave him some second thoughts. Maybe that's what got him in trouble. I'm putting the posters for these two men close together on the bulletin board because both of them saw what they had to do, and they did it, and they were honest about it."

The two were shocked. "You must hate Robert E. Lee!"

"Stuff it!" I shut them down.

On one corner of the poster for Lee was a small photo of him. Later that day, as I prepared to leave for home, I glanced at it. Words from a letter Lee wrote to his wife came to mind. He had been so sick that winter, and now, in spring, he spotted a place where some forest violets had burst into bloom.

Unfortunately, they got caught by a late frost. The humble bed of violets resembled a splendid display of diamonds, glittering in the woods. Lee wrote to his wife about how beautiful and yet how cruel nature (and war) could be, and he added these words:

Though age with its winters has whitened my head, and its frosts have hardened my bones, my heart, you well know, is not hardened to you, and summer returns when I see you.

I knew how gallant Lee was about his family women, and how when he heard of his daughter's death, he sat in his tent and wept.

Had I done the right thing, putting the Christian next to the Muslim? I had no respect for Muslim treatment of women, and no respect for that religion's association with slavery. It was Muslims who marched African captives to the coast and sold them to slavers. Did Jess completely understand the X he wore?

I left that evening full of doubt, wondering if I'd done the right thing.

*

It was 4:30 in the morning, and all of us seventh and eighth grade teachers were at the school, standing on the bus loading area. Mac The Principal, a long-time believer in field trips, arranged for us to take our students to the Smithsonian in D.C. Each of us was lining up in front of our assigned bus with the ten or so students on our list.

It promised to be a long day with our arrival back at the school late at night. Mac had alerted us about other places he wanted us to visit around the mall, including the Museum of Art and the tiny Walter Reed medical building. I had some reservations about the world of art, for I was sure there would be paintings and statues of naked men and woman, bad news for us teachers.

But Mac had a point about expanding our students' view of the world. We were short on culture but long on clans in our area. We had families living on the land and working it, and they weren't much interested in anything else. Amish families took their children out of the public schools around the seventh or eighth grades; after that, their lives were centered on work, not attending school.

Already Mr. Bontleger (not his real name) had come to school to see me and discuss the field trip long before it came about. What he wanted was this: his children were not to see any "dee-no-sars." He didn't believe in any of that old bones stuff, and he didn't want them believing in it, either. So I promised him that his boy and girl would stick with me, and I would make sure they didn't see any dinosaurs. I also made sure they were on my list of students.

I was in a good mood because neither Shrimp nor Buddy was on that list. In fact, only one student from my slow section was, and that was Tim, the quietest student of all. This might be a pleasant trip.

Mac wasn't in a good mood, however. Someone had slipped into his unlocked office and erased all that was recorded on the precious tape on which he had each of us teachers come to his office and speak through his recorder. We told what we taught, why we liked it, and how thankful we were for Mac's guidance. He had us prattle on for five minutes, and some of us went on and on for more than that. It was a good move on Mac's part. He planned to take that recording to the next school board meeting. There, he and the board members could drink coffee and listen to us teachers. They could talk about us and enjoy an evening of gossip.

And now someone had ruined that by erasing the tape. Mac was furious. That tape would have taken up the entire time for the board meeting.

That ashen-faced Bob was the villain, all of us were certain. He was next to me at the head of his line of students. "Mac said if he could prove it was me, he'd fire me on the spot, and he meant it," Bob said. For a moment, I was tempted to tell him I heard he'd recorded the William Tell Overture in place of the teachers' talking. But he was scared—and it wasn't true—and we were starting to board the buses.

One problem awaiting between us and Washington was Charles County, the seat of all sorts of corruption and gambling the Amish wouldn't like. Not all our students had brought snacks, and there were no bathrooms on our county school buses, so we had to stop now and then, and wherever we stopped—whether it was a convenience store, a bus stop, or a grocery store—the students were treated to the sight of people playing the slot machines. And as we arrived at the parking area of the Smithsonian, our tiny yellow buses were joined by sleek, towering commercial buses whose amused students laughingly looked down on us and made rude gestures. It wasn't a good start.

And it got worse at once for me. Once inside the Smithsonian, Tim turned into a monster. "Gawd," he exclaimed when he saw an escalator. He rode up and down on it over and over till I finally caught him coming down and yanked him off. But some wild side of his personality had been released, and he wasn't becoming quiet Tim again, not today he wasn't. He singlehandedly stopped and herded my group into a circle around some poor man who'd either had a heart attack or fainted, and from then on, I wasn't exactly leading the group. I was somewhere near the rear, trying to catch up with Tim. The Amish father needn't have worried—we passed by the dinosaur displays zip-a-dee-do-dah. Tim had a taste for the horrible, the altars where people had died and the knives used to kill them, shrunken heads, and frightening pagan idols. Sometimes my group passed another school's group going in the other direction, and self-pitying glances were exchanged between me and the other chaperone trying to keep up.

When Tim again formed our group into a circle, I feared another tourist was down, and I surged to the fore, herding the two Amish students with me. This time, as Tim and the other students scattered, we three saw before us, behind glass, a pornographic idol whose arms and legs were widespread, whose tongue hung from its gaping jaws down to its waist, and whose penis hung from its hips down to the floor ... no, actually it was dragging, flung out behind itself. For a moment, the two Amish children and I stared, fascinated. Whatta guy. Better than any dinosaurs.

I took advantage of this stop and got in the lead again. We had a frantic lunch, and there was an angry moment when Tim had to be collected ... he was throwing life savers on some sort of pendulum that proved the earth's rotation as it moved back and forth. And then, at last, with everyone present and in line, we headed for the minerals and jewels where I hoped to see the Hope Diamond on display.

We never got to see it. Some sort of folding metal grating, like a baby barrier, was preventing us from entering. A dark, angry face on the other side of that grillwork told me in no uncertain terms we weren't to enter. He said he didn't care if we called "Snick, Core, or the Double N Double A-C-P." He didn't give a damn. We weren't coming in. What's more, he hoped we would *Never* come to the Smithsonian again. He may have said *never* twice. The cameras that were supposed to be focused on the Hope Diamond weren't doing that anymore. Some students had jumped up and hit them so they were turned every whichaway except in the right direction. Some of the boys had scruffed their feet on the carpet and then touched the guards, causing the guards to suffer an electrical shock.

After that, there was another short stop to collect Tim again. He'd discovered a freight elevator and was about to take a trip up in it.

The Museum of Art was just as horrible as I thought it would be. Tim thought a statue of Hermes was hilarious. He regaled it with hoots and whoops of laughter. I tried reminding Tim that surely he'd seen not just himself but other male family members with no clothes on, but Tim insisted that if a feller was "nick-ed" he had no business wearing a hat. For Tim, "nick-ed" meant all the way or nothing. From then on, Tim's presence was no secret, for his noises every time he saw some woman or man "nick-ed" let me know exactly where he was.

At the Reed medical building, it only got worse. There wasn't any bathroom in there, and three people ended up being overwhelmed by the horrible things shown. They sat outside on the steps. Tim wasn't one of the three.

I was.

Back inside our bus, we had to wait for all the buses to be loaded and every student to be accounted for, of course. While we waited, our bus was rocking back and forth crazily as the students went from one side to the other following the movements of a creature they found absolutely captivating. What was it?

A squirrel.

I got a crashing headache. On the way back, a girl fell asleep with her head on my shoulder, and I let her stay there, sleeping. A few days later, she came down with measles. Shortly after that, so did I.

In those days, doctors came to your house to take care of you. My doctor informed me that a thing like measles could cause hardships when an older person like me came down with it. I was in my early thirties then, and I felt insulted that he called me "older." It was even worse when it turned out he was right.

The Amish children didn't get to see any dinosaurs.

*

At first, it was a little girl who named our tomcat Mr. Mousie Motoe, but we were too lazy for all that, and it got shortened to Mr. Motoe. He was an affectionate cat who felt responsible for us ... I say that because it was his habit to leave small offerings at our front door: birds, squirrels, mice, baby rabbits. He offered up whatever he found and left them there for us, sometimes dead and sometimes not. He was offended when we took—no, snatched—a screaming critter away from him. His angry eyes when he lost his prey were memorable.

The message those eyes sent was this: *What's the matter with you people? I'm just trying to help you. If I were a tiger, you would be in real trouble right now. And when you put me down, I'm going to bite your legs.*

You know about this, I think, because a man's eyes do the same thing when he sees something that gives him pleasure, something he wants to pursue, to capture. The darkest part of the eye gets larger and larger till it's filled all the space it can ... and then it's *pounce*. Large, dark eyes ... and threatening.

What that tomcat was saying was this:

I'll never change, never. You'll always be pitiful you, but I'll be Me!

I mention this because when I think of the student I'll call John, I think of our tomcat. Not that they were alike, for they weren't.

John came up to my desk one autumn day at the end of the last period. He asked for my help. He wanted me to drive him home, to be his spokesperson and protector. He was afraid of his grandmother, for God's sake.

Four times I drove John back to where he and his younger brother George were living at their grandparents' house. Each time I talked with his grandmother. The boys' mother and their grandmother were at war with each other. It must have been a serious argument. The mother, banished, wasn't around. I learned the younger boy, George, didn't look at all like her. He was treated well. John, on the other hand, looked a lot like the daughter the grandmother detested. He was treated unfairly.

I sensed what John might be thinking. My husband and I had no children. John never asked, but I imagined he might be wishing for it: how about taking *him* in, then.

Even before I mentioned that possibility to my husband, I think I knew what his answer was going to be. It was no.

The student was artistic, intelligent, a good guy. What tugged at my heart was the way this young one knew he needed help. I've always been a dedicated rescuer. *To the rescue!* It was my heart's cry every time. Yet I was helpless.

There was a smugness about her when the grandmother talked about how sweet dear George was, and there was a certain look on her face when she talked about John that unsettled me. I reminded her that she'd told me how John was like her daughter, and when I asked if she might be punishing John because of that resemblance, she shrugged. Was that saying *So? So what?* Only once was the grandfather there when I was, and he sat silently.

John probably saw there was no help coming from anyone. So one day he rode his bicycle up to the youth detention center and asked them to take him in. He told them he would do some things to cause his arrest if they refused—which was what they did at first, after they got over their surprise that any boy would come and ask to be put in such a place. When the public became aware of John and his request, it caused a fuss, and then the detention center took him in. I tried to get some art supplies sent to him, but I was turned away. Weeks went by with John held at the detention center.

I think it was about that time I started pulling weeds till after dark because I didn't want to go into the house. There was a cold silence there.

I ended up involved in discussions with family court officials, and then there were hearings. My testimony went, more or less, like this:

J (judicial official): How many times did you visit John's home and talk with the grandmother?
M (me): Well, four, if you count the last one as a visit.
J: How was John being treated?
M: Unfairly. From what I could see, and from what John told me, his younger brother was never punished, but John always was. I saw John as well behaved, but his grandmother said he was evil because of his connection to his mother and the way he looked like her.
J: What are some examples of unfair treatment?
M: Well, she took them to the beach one day, and when they got wet, she was angry. The younger brother George wasn't punished, but John was. He had to go without supper. Both of them got wet.
J: Why would she be angry if they got wet at the beach?
M: I asked her that. She said they were supposed to play only on the sand.
J: Other things?
M: For one thing, John told me George never has any chores to do, but John has lots of them. Once he forgot to take the trash out to their burn pit. All his art supplies were taken away from him for months.
J: Are you sure the other brother has no chores?
M: It looked that way to me, and John said that was the case. I know that at one visit I made, I saw George laughing

at John as John was doing some assigned thing, I think bringing in kindling wood.

J: Why do you think this student confided in you?

M: I guess he didn't see help from anywhere else. He ended up kicking his grandmother's air conditioner out of her bedroom window—

J: He did what?

M: He kicked her air conditioner out of her second-story bedroom window. It fell to the ground below and was ruined. That's what she said.

The questioner looked unhappy.

M: Well, if you're scared of her, but you depend on her for everything, you can't attack her, so her air conditioner was just fair game. That's the way I see it, the way I think he saw it.

J: How was he punished for that?

M: He was chained to his bed for the weekend and the following Monday. He had a slop jar and drinking water, and he had food brought to him. He fed himself with his free hand. And at night, he slept in the bed, still with his one hand chained.

J: And how do you know this is true?

M: Well, certainly I know he was absent that Monday. After John told me, I went there again, and when I asked her about it, she said he deserved it. She was aggressive, and I got a little scared of her myself. It was after that John went to the detention center. And the last time I tried to talk to her, she refused to talk to me.

The grandmother was sitting there, nearby. I didn't look at her. Instead, I stared at the treetops out the courthouse windows.

I think it was being chained that carried the day for John.

The woman who drove the school bus that picked John up each day and dropped him off after school thought so much of him, she and her husband wanted to take him into their large, happy family. In the end, that is what happened, and it was a good thing for him.

After the deposition I left the third floor. I stopped off at the second floor for a bit, and then I went to the elevator to go down to the first floor.

When the elevator doors opened, there, in that elevator, all alone, was the grandmother. As soon as I saw her face, her eyes, I knew what had been bothering me all along about her. I had seen those dark-filled eyes before, every time some poor helpless thing was taken away from Mr. Motoe. Her tense body and her fierce gaze told me she felt superior to me in every way and would never change, *never*, and I decided at once I could walk down one flight of stairs as easy as pie.

*

I'd taught night classes before—and enjoyed it—teaching those seeking a high school diploma. Now I took on the job of teaching another night class. I was to teach English and basic skills to Haitian new-comers to America.

Maybe I thought they'd be sacrificing chickens on the hood of my car. Couldn't have been more wrong. What I found were cheerful, polite people, smiling and kind. I don't know if I could have been so cooperative, if I were in a strange new place, not understanding everything. They insisted on calling me "Teacher," no other name, even though I made a point of giving them my last name. I took this as a mark of respect, because I sensed it was intended that way.

Right from the start, they struggled with American expressions that had no literal meaning. For example, if you said, "I was at the mall, and guess who I ran across," they thought an accident happened. Fortunately, I quickly caught on to their musical nature. Just about anything could be taught to the tune of "You Are My Sunshine." If we could sing it, they got it. We sang about money, making change, paying rent, about what a verb does, how quotation marks looked like little hummingbird feet; we sang our way through everything. All the topics I was supposed to cover were disappearing, checked off, right on schedule.

I sang "The Star-Spangled Banner" to them and the pledge of allegiance. They didn't like our national anthem. It was, they said, too hard to sing. Theirs was better. They sang it to me, and I agreed; theirs was better. But, I told them, the best anthem of all was "Waltzing Matilda" for Australia. I explained what the words meant, and they liked it, but still, they said, theirs was best of all. I explained the background of ours, how the poor doctor was held below deck, how he kept asking if the flag was still flying, how a rooster flew to the top of the fort and crowed, thinking it was dawn with the explosions taking place. They liked the story, but theirs was still best. They sang their anthem to me again.

I was beginning to pick up some of their patter, how to say "Good evening," and, "How are you?" If I had seen them more regularly, I might have become conversant. The problem was they weren't regular in their attendance. Their jobs and their children came first, of course, and so sometimes they were there, sometimes not.

One evening when I took attendance, I wondered aloud about Jean Pierre's absence. He was one of the few who came regularly. Did anyone know why Jean wasn't there?

"Oh," one of his fellow workers volunteered, "he cannot come tonight. Today at work, he fuck up."

It was inevitable they would pick up our roughest words. I had to deal with it. "That word *fuck* is not to be used around women and children. It's a word used by men under stress, in a locker room, on athletic fields, around other men. If you use that word around your employer, your boss, he won't be happy with you."

I had their attention. "But he did, he did … he did fuck up."

"No matter. You have to understand. Don't use that word, no matter what he did or didn't do."

Eyes were downcast, and there was some confused mutterings. "But he did … he did …"

I was running out of patience. I spent a little time lecturing them on how I meant what I said.

"But, teacher, he lose everything he eat."

A light came on in my brain. "Wait a minute. Are you trying to say Jean Pierre *up-chucked*? That he threw up all the food he ate?"

Up-chucked! Yes, that was it exactly! There was a sort of celebration. One more American expression understood! Up-chucked ! Most excellent expression!

And then, a silence. I could almost hear them wrapping their minds around a question. All those eyes were fastened on me. Okay, so that took care of that deal *up-chucked*. Now, what about that word *fuck*? What was it exactly that made that word so offensive, teacher? Please explain.

That was when I realized some things can't be taught to the tune of "You Are My Sunshine."

*

When Jamie moved us to South Florida, life became hectic as soon as I began teaching at one of the crowded middle schools. There were about five thousand new students arriving in that county each year, and new buildings were going up fast to catch up with it. Portable classrooms sprang up, as was the case with the new school where I was teaching. The portables surrounded everything almost as soon as the main building opened.

Many students came from foreign places. Parents had businesses in more than one country with residences in each. Students came to live with family members who were U.S. citizens; others fled to our country from some oppressive place. The first day I spotted a boy who wore a tee shirt that had printed across its front CCCP (the Union of Soviet Socialist Republics). When I asked him where he got that, he said he got it in Moscow where he was born. In the back of the room was a lanky German youth who was living with kin so he could attend school in the same area where he could sharpen ice hockey skills. A delicate Asian girl with her family had sneaked out of North Korea into South Korea and somehow ended up in South Florida. A boy from Shanghai sat near another Asian boy, one who came into my class a couple of weeks late with his parents escorting him. They were coming from communist mainland China (when I jokingly asked, "Wouldn't they let you out? Ha, ha," I got a look that told me I was way out of line). The student who had a Brazilian father (speaking Portuguese) and a Chinese mother was fluent in English, Chinese, and Portuguese, which indicated he was a lot smarter than I was.

There were plenty of American students who moved into that county. A boy from Arkansas was sent to live with relatives so he could train at a nearby swimming and diving center. Others had parents who had been transferred to the area. They were coming from small towns out west or up north where custom was still king and rules were cheerfully obeyed. They were the saddest. We've underestimated how hard it is for a student to move from a place where he or she feels happy to another where everything is strange and frightening.

*

In Hot Florida, Testing

If this child has darkened the slot indicating
his question mark outside the quotation marks
instead of inside the quotation marks (as is correct
in this case), at least he knew question marks
and quotation marks but if
the machine humming and clicking has no
little holes and no little slots and no allowances
for almost right and very close and if
the child somehow remembers a long-ago father
whose blood flowed in his before-that father and
whose blood flows
in him, standing on his long-ago porch full of
satisfaction that his wheat was good
and a long-ago mother whose blood flowed in his before-that mother
whose blood flows in him, in her long-ago garden
full of iris and peonies and thyme, so that he
chews on his pencil in the traffic, in the sand,
and
marks, marks, almost right
almost caring, almost knowing
sycamores and owls in him
snow drifting deep loam
and smell of lilacs in him geese
calling cattle and horses stomping in him
all these things he cannot see or touch now
in him
does the machine measure that?

*

In South Florida I had to win, each day, the respect once given to me freely. Before, students sat quietly and allowed me to call the roll and start the lesson. Now, I had to have material on the board for them to copy as soon as they came into the room, a sort of excuse to remain quiet.

Before, I had students who, for religious reasons, couldn't pledge allegiance to the flag, but they listened to me when I advised them to just stand up when we had the pledge, not to say anything, not to put a hand over the heart, and no one would notice or say anything. Now, in South Florida, there were quite a few who refused to even stand, who continued their conversations with other students (sometimes in a language other than English), and who, still sitting, turned their backs on me. They dismissed me as if I were some servant when I tried to get them to cooperate.

I, who had always fancied myself to be a rescuer, was now in need of being rescued. The student who planted herself at the end of the cafeteria line asking students for their money, refused even to acknowledge my presence when I tried to stop her from doing that. I had to go get an administrator to move her away from there. And, of course, she went right back again as soon as he moved away.

Some of the new and yuppy rich let me know who they were right away. In conferences with them, I would be asked if I knew where they lived (always some exclusive development), and did I know who they were, and how old was I anyway. Clearly, they wanted me to be master of subject matter and a style setter as well. My peasant preferences weren't appreciated. I have always loved baskets, for example; they are one thing not made by machine. I liked carrying my papers in one of my widest old baskets. My grade-level administrator, spotting me with my basket, sidled up to me and inquired, with a sly grin, "Goin' berry pickin'?" He also told me if I ever got a more presentable car—something that didn't make his stomach churn every time he saw it in the school parking lot—he was going to go home and have a stiff drink.

Jamie gave me a briefcase. Then he thought it was a good idea to get a better car. I loved my car, the Chief, with its headband of Indian characters around its roof, getting its nine miles per gallon. Its back left-side passenger door was liable to pop open when I made a right turn (at some time in its history, something must have run into the Chief's rear). No problem, for you simply tied your rear passengers in, running rope from the handle of the right rear door over to the left. Quick solution.

I found a note that had fallen from a desk onto the floor: "Here she stands," it read, "wearing a dress my mother wouldn't use as a cleaning rag." That hurt. If I couldn't be a teacher, I would have liked being a cowboy, or maybe Lena Horne. If I couldn't have the Chief, I would have liked a purple Prowler, or maybe a 1933 Ford coupe … but people kept insisting I must meet their standards, not my own. I began feeling inadequate.

One time at a dog show, I stood next to an old guy who looked like a bum. I commented to him that the fellow in the ring with a dog being shown must have a lot of dogs because he was in the ring so often. The gentleman told me this was a professional handler, and that the owners of that dog weren't even in attendance, that the handler took dogs all over the country. Wow, said I, it must be nice to have that much money. He agreed.

"Yes," he said, "it is." Strange answer.

Turned out this run-down, affable fellow was a DuPont. My kind of rich guy. No fuss or feathers He handled wealth with never a care. But the rich of South Florida cared. Or they put their kids in private schools. One Japanese dad, who had a business near Miami, came to a conference to tell me he was pulling his daughter out of the public schools. He would be putting her into a private school that had more Asian students … because, he explained, white Americans eat too much beef and drink too much milk, and it makes them smell funny. So my basket didn't suit, my car didn't suit, my dress didn't suit, and now I eat the wrong stuff, and I stink.

*

I gave up on field trips. Going or coming back, our students wanted the buses to stop at shopping centers. At plays, laser lights appeared flashing across the actors' faces. I gave up.

However, because it was to be the school's first yearbook and I was in charge of it, I took my yearbook editors to a meeting with the publisher. I loaded the three of them, one in the front and two in the back seat of the Chief, and off we went. The assistant principal, I'm told, tried to stop me out in the parking lot, but I was already out the drive. It seems there were insurance and permission papers I was supposed to fill out and sign, and I hadn't done that.

If he ever knew I had two students tied in on the back seat, he might have gone for that stiff drink he talked about. I never heard, so I guess it went unnoticed. However, I forgot, one day, to set the emergency brake, and the Chief rolled into the center of the parking lot. I certainly heard about that, for the car was located in such a spot it was on display. There was a big reaction. So Jamie convinced me it was time to get rid of the Chief, and we sold it to a fellow who took it to the islands, where, I suppose, it was used to haul hemp or chickens … who knows what. What a horrible fate for the Chief.

*

One of the worst things is the repeated stuff, for it goes on and on, over and over, till the brain goes numb. The university sent me a young woman to mentor. She had a mind to become a teacher. That is, she did till she saw I was teaching the same lesson over to each class, five times a day, and if I taught six classes, six times. She turned in the book I'd given her and fled. She said they should be put in some auditorium and taught all at the same time. Talk about a scheduling problem.

In quite another way, my life was boring stuff. Like Marley's ghost, I dragged boxes of papers with me wherever I went. It didn't work if I asked Jamie to help check answers. He would write insulting things on the students' papers ("Do you want to spend the rest of your life in 8th grade?"), and I would have to use white-out to cover what he'd written, both sides of the paper (for students can read stuff backwards when they see something from the other side of the paper). Jamie did that knowing I would never ask him to help again. I resorted to Lily, a widow who lived across the street. I figured she could use some extra money, so I offered to pay her if she would help check some papers, thus lightening my load. For a while that worked. Then my papers started coming back to me smelling like bourbon. Lily had a problem, and checking my papers caused her to fall off the wagon. It got so bad I couldn't stand anything that repeated itself over and over.

So, son, I am sincerely sorry for what I did to your guitar.

*

I've never been good about getting down on my knees beside the bed to pray. I think it's because I'm so used to small monkey sighs (prayers) of thankfulness, I don't want to ask God for help with problems I create for myself, things I shouldn't blame

God for. Now, I found myself on my knees asking for favors. If you don't mind, God, help.

For one thing, if you have any success with discipline problems, what you will get next year will be twice as many of those, or maybe one of the worst. We had in our school a student who was so bad he just walked out of his classes whenever he felt like it and went about the main building doing outlandish things. Sometimes he prowled around the portables, too, and on one occasion he threw a rock into an open portable door, hitting a girl in the leg. Seems strange, but the mother of this evil-doer threatened to sue. She said somebody should have stopped him from doing bad things. In response, the school board hired somebody to follow the boy around, recording the things he did. I had taught the boy's sister with some success. Now, at the end of the year, that girl told me her mother was going to ask the administration to give her brother to me next year. Her mother felt sure he and I would get along well together.

Perhaps he and I would get along well together if I had a complete personality change and we were planning a bank robbery or a murder. With one casual sentence, his sister ruined my summer break, putting me on my knees on a regular basis at night, asking for divine intervention.

At the same time, as the year ended, there was danger of another sort. A student had decided he could force me into passing him in spite of flunked tests and work not turned in. My car was keyed, the new—well, used, but almost new—car, and a bouquet of flowers was turned upside down over my desk, water and flowers all over the paperwork I had there. Some of his friends stopped by my room during my planning period, letting me know they knew where I lived. I muddled along anyway, doing what I felt was the right thing, but it took its toll. Sometimes teachers, I'm convinced, wake up in the middle of the night, wondering what else, earlier in their lives, they could have chosen to do. They don't sleep well because they're facing the fact that a teacher in his or her fifties doesn't have many other choices … except sticking to it, hoping for the best. And asking God for help. God help the teacher whose health and resolve begin to slip away.

As mine were.

*

I agreed to teach another night class. I had success before doing that, and I had enjoyed those classes.

This class was different. When I entered the room that first night, I was startled at how many people there were. There must have been thirty-five or forty people. Unlike the Haitian class I had taught, these people were from many different countries. I was told they spoke English (sort of), but I should expect there would be some who didn't. The names on the roll call sheet looked difficult, and I spotted names of countries that looked like everywhere except Greenland. I remember noticing "Estonia" and wondering where in the world was that place. I began calling the roll, tentatively.

Almost at once a woman stood up and exclaimed something in a foreign language. She was loud and sounded like a machinegun. A man sitting next to her also stood up. "She says you talk too fast," he explained.

What? I hadn't even started talking. Surely my attempt to call the roll couldn't be called "too fast." The woman's complaint rattled me. Maybe I had better put something up for them to copy. For this class, there was a sort of "script" to follow, probably a means of making sure everything actually got taught. I had pens to use for the whiteboard and pages of material for them to copy and for me to cover. Let's put up some of that.

I turned to the whiteboard and used the whiteboard pens I'd been given to write material there. I got a lot written, and then it dawned on me I wasn't writing on any whiteboard. I was writing (with a PEN) on the pulled-down movie screen. The room fell silent. I turned around, and I could see the doubt on their faces: *is she supposed to do that thing she's doing there?* I got even more rattled, and I pulled up the screen. Then it occurred to me I must use the overhead projector, then, to have them copy material. So now I pulled the screen down again. The faces of my audience said to me: *first she writes on it and then she pulls it up and now she's pulling it down and is she sane?*

I addressed the man who spoke English, asking him to explain I made a mistake, and now I wanted them to copy the work from the overhead projector. I had overhead sheets, same material as for the whiteboard. So now I put one of those sheets on the projector and turned it on.

"I know I messed up the screen," I told the English speaker, "but tell them, please, to do the best they can to copy this work while I call the roll." He spoke, and some of them seemed to understand him, and some seemed to understand me. There was some grumbling (after all, the material to be copied was right on top of what I'd written on the screen, so it was a scrambled mess). But at least they were quietly copying.

I almost made it through the roll call. Suddenly there was a real uproar. It took me by surprise. They were yelling at me, for God's sake. The man who spoke English finally jumped up, put his hands on my shoulders and turned me toward the overhead projector. There was smoke coming from it.

There was an evacuation of the classroom, and how the rest of the evening went I remember only vaguely. I do remember telling Susan, who was in charge of the night classes, that I had ruined the movie screen and would pay for it, and the overhead projector might be ruined, too, and I wasn't going to pay for that, and I quit.

That was my last attempt at night class. An inglorious effort, if ever there was one.

*

I was big sister and mentor, appointed to help Barry during his first year of teaching at our school. He didn't need much help from me. He was a tall, relaxed guy with a big grin, at ease with everyone, including his students. He loved to eat, and I teased him, saying I knew he'd been in the faculty cafeteria room because when I got there, most of the food was gone. He threatened to sing, and those of us who had heard him do that begged him not to. He was a big fan of *The Hobbit*, and he played basketball.

After his time with us, Barry moved on to another school, and he soon became established and popular there.

And then came that last day of school.

Last day is stressful, anyway, with students bidding one another goodbye and wasting time. In my class, the boy from Shanghai was sad because his family and he would be going back there, and the girl from Turkey was in tears because her family was going back and she would have to wear the traditional female Muslim garb. The students who had been so loose-handed about living in America, I noticed, were not so happy about leaving. At Barry's school, some students got into trouble in the cafeteria, and Nate, a boy Barry taught, was among those. The assistant principal on duty in the cafeteria that day suspended some of the students and sent them home. Nate was among those.

Nate argued about having to leave and go home, but it didn't do any good. The administrator held him to it, and so

Nate left, but he asked that man what time he himself would be leaving that day. I guess the assistant principal thought an adult might show up to speak for Nate, so he told him he would be leaving at 4:00.

At home, Nate went where the man who lived with his grandmother had a gun hidden. Nate took that loaded gun, and now, as the last period of the school day approached, he rode his bicycle back onto the school grounds bringing the loaded weapon with him. Maybe he intended to confront the assistant principal with it.

As he entered the building, he came first upon Barry's room. There were some girls in that classroom Nate wanted to talk to, so he knocked on the door and asked to speak to them. Barry let the girls go to the open door to be with Nate for a while. When Barry went to the door and told Nate he had to close it now, and Nate had to leave, Nate pulled the gun on him.

Barry had time to say, 'Nate, don't point that gun at me."

Nate shot and killed his teacher. A distant security camera showed it clearly, Nate shooting Barry in the head, and then with the weapon following Barry's body as it fell to the floor. And it makes no sense, of course. Why would a student come to school seeking one man he disliked and shoot another one he liked, just because a door had to be closed? I can only suppose Nate was taken up in the pretense of being a tough-guy secret agent, something he wanted to be, and Barry got in his way. So Barry, who rode his bike to work so as not to pollute the air by driving a car, whose flower garden displayed flowers butterflies especially liked, and who had a young family, died on the last day of school, last period of that day, because Nate stopped by to talk to some girls. I heard later that while in jail, Nate wrote to the Secret Service asking if he could still, some distant day, become a Secret Service agent.

After Barry's death, I found myself wondering how it was that I was still around. The assistant principal who disliked the Chief so much died of cancer. The chic female assistant principal who advised me not to reveal my age to the principal was also dead from cancer. Our principal wanted her staff to be capable and young—or so we all thought. The principal left our school and headed to another state where she clashed with a strong teachers' union. Bob, the jokester from my earliest days of teaching, dropped dead on the golf course. My former husband was dead, and my second was ill. What in the world was I doing still hobbling around? It was time to quit the whole shebang.

The last day, students in the classroom next door wanted to know my age (I was in my classroom, planning period). The last five minutes, on a slip of paper, I sent that information to them. There had been conversation in that room before my age arrived. Now, the classroom fell silent. *What?* the silence said. *She can't be that old.* Sure I could.

The year was 2000, and I was 67. I had spent forty-five years teaching, half of that in the rural mid-Atlantic and half in the crowded semi-tropical south Florida. I earned $3,000 a year when I started teaching. I thought I was rich.

The changes in education I'd seen were mind-stretching. I remember the mother of the Arkansas boy asking me on the phone, "Are you telling me you have an armed police officer patrolling your school?" As a matter of fact, we had two, and occasionally we had a drug dog as well. The lockers and book cubicles were done away with (much too handy as storing places for drugs), and so everyone had backpacks and wheeled luggage. I saw increased use of recording and camera-ready phones. I saw pants so low the crotch was around the knees, and so-called dancing that looked obscene. Some students began announcing themselves as bi-sexual.

One mother came to a conference to tell me I wasn't stylish enough to be a role model for her daughter. She brought with her to the meeting her live-in boyfriend. Her occupation? Marriage counselor. Another came to tell me I was in the wrong when I made her son turn inside out his tee shirt that displayed male genitalia. "He has rights," she said. Her occupation? Guidance counselor. Another came to a meeting with the craziest piece of hair sticking up like a celery stalk at the top of her head. Hair stylist.

*

I thought of Bob the jokester from my earliest days of teaching the other morning as I was stirring my coffee. Mac The Principal hated all the spoons teachers took from the cafeteria up to the cramped faculty room. There they stirred the coffee they made or brought up to the room.

    Every day, those spoons would be sitting on the window sill. Mac would gather them up and take them back to the cafeteria, making sarcastic comments about those lazy slobs who weren't responsible enough to return their spoons to the right place. Somehow Bob found an outlet that sold cheap spoons much like ours. Just before he left for the day, or sometime during the last period, Bob would slip into the faculty room and put spoons on that window sill. He always left more spoons than we had faculty. He knew it was driving Mac nuts.

    Mac was bald, and Bob found one of those silly jokester Valentines, one that folded up, and when it unfolded, it showed a bald head with the words, "You should get ahead, you need one" printed beneath. Around Valentine's Day, he would leave that, folded up, or something like it, on the window sill underneath the spoons.

Now, when I'm sitting around feeding the birds, I have a prayer I send up to God. It's not long, because if it was, I would probably fall asleep thinking it:

Father in Heaven, please favor and protect the rascals, the jokesters, the comics, the jesters, the ones who make us smile, who make us laugh at every self-important, political thing. They need help most of all because they help so many others. That's not a monkey prayer; it just comes from a monkey. Please remember them.
Me, Ingrid
Amen

Running on the Rail

There are horses that look so splendid and strong
As they pose or they prance up a storm.
There are horses who wheeze and pretend they can't run
So they have to be pushed to perform.

There are even a few who resist to the last
A rider at all on the back,
Who'll toss off a jockey and take off alone,
Running amok on the track.

Yet the horse who's not handsome
But who's been around
Saves some strength, when the others might fail,
And he'll bring you around in a good frame of mind
'Cause he knows how to cling to the rail.

And we're that kind of horse, although sometimes it seems
That the others—well, we seem to trail 'em.
Just wait for an opening and then at the end,
In the last desperate furlong, we'll nail 'em.
Yes, we know we're not handsome, we know we're not young.
Still, the fact is, we're glad we're not frail
For we're older and tougher, and when things get rougher,
We know how to run on the rail.

The End

Made in the USA
Las Vegas, NV
05 May 2023

71594568R00044